I0477777

THE RULES HAVE CHANGED

www.FreeScenarioReview.com

Chris Brown (NMLS #303797)

321.696.9696

Chris@OrlMtgPro.com

1331 S International Pkwy Suite #2251

Lake Mary, FL 32746

Equal Housing Opportunity/Lender

"Home is the nicest word there is."

- Laura Ingalls Wilder

"It is never the wrong time to meet the right people or get the right advice."

- Chris Brown

Table of Contents

1. Know the Difference Between Different Types Of Homes You Can Purchase

When you're buying a home and you're going out looking at purchasing your own place, it's helpful to know the different types of properties that exist.

There are four main types of properties.

Each one has positives and negatives and we're going to go over the different types of homes you can purchase.

Single Family Home

The first is a single-family home. This is the most common type of home. It's what you're used to seeing in a neighborhood where it's a detached home usually with a garage and there's going to be space in between each house.

This is the most common type of home purchase in America.

It's the kind of place that people will purchase when they think about the American Dream, but it is not the only type of property.

There are other types of homes that work for different types of people as well.

Condos

The second kind of property is a Condo. A Condo is similar to an apartment but everybody in the complex owns their unit.

In a condo you own everything 'inside your walls'. Everything 'outside your walls' is either common space, owned by somebody else, or belongs to the complex itself.

When you own a condo, you're going to have a condominium association fee every month.

These fees will cover things like your amenities, taking care of the parking lots, security, and things like that.

Condos are great for people who want to be in a close environment but have the security of ownership.

Townhomes

The third type of property that's available is a townhome.

A townhome is like a condo in that you have shared walls, but with a townhome you own everything inside of your unit as well as the front and back of it.

You typically have *some* property with a townhome.

Most townhomes are going to be two stories with a small front yard and a small backyard.

Occasionally, you will see townhome complexes that also have garages.

Duplex

The fourth type of property is a duplex.

A duplex is a unit that has two homes attached in the middle.

So typically if you own a duplex, you're going to own the 'both' units. In some areas you may be able to buy only one half of the duplex.

You would own everything inside your unit as well as your yard with one shared wall with your neighbor.

2. Ask to See Any Homeowners Association Documents Before You Make an Offer or During Your Inspection Period

It's important to know what's required before you buy into a neighborhood. Every homeowner's association or HOA is a little bit different in what they allow and what they don't allow.

They also have different requirements of the homeowners and different association dues and you want to know all these things before you move into a neighborhood.

Let's say for example you own a motorhome and it's important to you to be able to park that at your house. You want to read the HOA documents to make sure that's an option.

Some neighborhoods don't allow motorhomes and you must put it in storage. So that's one example of why it's important to get all the Homeowner's Association documents before you make an offer.

If that's not possible you can review the documents during your inspection period. You will have the ability to get out of the contract during the inspection period if you find something in the HOA docs you don't like.

3. Find Out If You Qualify for Any Special Financing Programs

One of the reasons it's important to talk with a lender before you start going out looking at houses is so you can know exactly which mortgage programs you qualify for and how much home you can afford based on the payment you want.

There are some special programs and government programs that make it easier for renters to become homeowners or for people to move up into new homes.

The **VA Loan Program** is one example.

VA stands for Veterans Administration and this is a loan that is available for most veterans and active duty military.

There are some requirements, so you'll want to speak with a Mortgage Loan Originator – like Chris - to make sure that you qualify. They can also help you get the Certificate of Eligibility from the VA showing that you qualify.

The VA loan is great because it doesn't require a down payment. It covers 100% of your loan amount.

In most cases it will save you several thousand dollars out-of-pocket since you can keep the down payment.

Another type of special program is the **FHA Loan**.

This was designed for first time homebuyers to be able to bring only a small down payment at closing.

In most cases, the FHA program only requires a 3.5% down payment compared to a normal conventional home loan that require more down payment.

The third government program that helps home buyers get into a house with little or no money out of pocket is the **USDA Program**.

This was designed for *rural* communities and typically is available in more country areas. You may be surprised as to what that covers so be sure to ask.

This program is great for those homebuyers because it also does not require a down payment and provides 100% financing.

The last kind of loan program we will cover here is the **conventional** loan.

A conventional loan is great for folks that have moderate credit or better. You used to have to put more down, but you can now put down as little as 5% or – if you are buying for the first time – as little as 3%. Yes, you read right... even less than FHA.

Comparing these options is a good idea and you can play 1001 'what-if' scenarios in the privacy of your own home by downloading the mortgage mobile APP – www.PocketMortgageAdvice.com

4. Be Prepared to Act Fast When You Find What You Want

What that means is not to delay putting an offer on a home when it meets your needs and you feel like it's the one for you.

Depending on the market, there is a good chance your offer will go up against other offers for the same home.

There's no reason to wait in getting your offer in as fast as possible to have the best chance at being the only one they're looking at.

When a seller receives an offer from a buyer, they have three options in what they can do:

1. They can accept the offer

They can take your offer exactly the way that it has been presented and they can execute the contract. This is rare

2. They can do nothing

The seller can receive your offer and they can never respond or even acknowledge that they received your offer. This really only occurs if you make an insulting low-ball offer.

There's no legal requirement for them to respond to your offer.

(Now obviously in most cases, the seller will respond, but understand it's not a requirement.)

3. They can counter your offer

Most common is a seller to counter your offer.

If they do counter, it could be based on price or on other terms of the contract, such as the earnest money amount, the title company, the closing day, the inspection period and things like that.

So again, it's important that when you find a house that you're interested in and you want to buy, that you move quickly to purchase that home.

5. Most Buyers' Agents Represent You for Free

We'll often get the question - how is it possible that home buyer agents can represent a buyer and not get paid?

Well, they do get paid.

Buyer's agents are paid by the listing agent.

When a person lists their home for sale, they sign a listing agreement with that agent.

The listing agreement will cover things like what is the listing price, how long are they going to work together and what the commission is.

So, let's say for example, the seller agrees to pay 6% commission. That listing broker gets to decide how to split the commission. They could keep 3% and offer 3% to the agent who represents the buyer.

The buyer's agent is being taken care of by the commission that the seller is paying.

6. Get Pre-Approved for A Home Loan Before You Start House Hunting

It's important before you go look for a house that you know what you are qualified for. Remember Chapter 4?

One of the worst feelings is to go and find the house of your dreams put in an offer that's accepted by the seller, only to find out a few weeks later that you don't qualify for that amount of house and that you'll need to go find a smaller home, this is why you should get pre-approved before you go out looking at houses.

Being pre-approved means that you will know *exactly* how much home you qualify for.

You'll know what payment to expect on homes and what price range you should consider so there'll be no surprises.

You'll know that any home you're agreeing to purchase will be within your budget and within your qualifications.

Pre-qualify here – www.FreeScenarioReview.com

7. Understand the Home Buying Process Before You Start

There are basically seven steps to buying a house you'll want to understand.

I'm going to share the process, so you will always know where you are at any given time once you start.

Step 1. Get Pre-Approved

We just talked about how important it is to get pre-approved, so you will know exactly how much home you're qualified for and what your payment will be on that house.

Being pre-approved will also strengthen the offers later when you go to write that contract because the seller will have confidence knowing you've already been pre-approved for the home loan.

Step 2. Find the House

Next, you're going to hire a real estate agent and they will help represent you in finding the perfect house for you. (For an agent referral, call Chris at the number in the footer of this page.)

Your Realtor has access to every home on the market and even houses that you might not be able to find on Zillow, Realtor.com or any other 3rd party websites.

These are called "pocket listings" so ask your real estate agent if they know of any.

Step 3. Write an Offer and Win a Contract

Once you find the house that you want to purchase, you're going to write an offer to that seller.

This is a OFFER, but it's only signed by you, not by the sellers yet.

On the offer, it's going to include the price, where and when you want to close, how much money you want to put up as a down payment and all the other parts of your offer are going to be listed in the contract.

It is called an Executed Contract once the seller accepts and signs it.

Step 4. Get a Home Inspection

You're going to hire a 3rd party independent inspector to come in and go through the house and tell you what they find out is right and wrong about the house. NOT ALL INSPECTIONS ARE CREATED EQUAL. Your agent can help you here.

Understand that it's the inspector's job to point out everything that's wrong and they will go over the house with a fine-tooth comb and point out every tiny imperfection but that does not mean the house is not worthy of you buying it.

You must really be purposeful with what you decide is important and fixable in the future during that inspection period.

Step 5. Home Appraisal

This will be ordered from your mortgage company, and again, an independent person will come out to the house that you're purchasing and agree on what the value of that house is.

If the value that the appraiser gives the house is above or equal to your contract price, then your mortgage company is going to give it the thumbs up.

If for some reason the home comes in at a lower value, either you'll need to renegotiate the contract, or you may need to pay the difference out-of-pocket. Of course, you can always walk-away.

Step 6. Receive Full Loan Approval

This will let you know that you've been completely approved and you're ready to go to closing.

Everything has been done in terms of researching your credit, income, and background. The mortgage company feels confident to provide you with a home loan.

This is also the time where the documents for your home loan and all the papers that you're going to have to sign are going to be drawn up and those are going to be sent to the closing company.

Step 7. Attend Closing & Become the Owner

Now it's time to attend closing, sign all the paperwork and you will officially become the new homeowner.

Closing is when you will provide your down payment and any other funds that you are paying at closing for any closing costs and other minor fees that come along with purchasing a home. Those will all be taken care of at closing.

8. Keep an Open Mind

When we say keep an open mind, what we want you to do is to know what's realistic for your budget.

If you have a $100,000 budget, that's going to purchase a different kind of home than a $300,000 budget and that budget will purchase a different home than a $500,000 budget.

Neither one of those is right or wrong, but you have to understand what's realistic for your price range.

One of the exercises that can be helpful is to do a needs-versus-wants sheet side-by-side.

Take a piece of paper and make one column for needs and one column for wants.

List out things like the bedrooms and bathrooms and different features and layouts and neighbor-hoods and all these things that you feel are important about the house that you're going to go shopping for.

Keep in mind what's a need versus a want, right?

A need may be that you need four bedrooms, but you want to have a three-car garage. You must decide which column each item fits in.

Also, there's a thing that we call the HGTV effect.

These shows about buying houses on HGTV have made some buyers not fully understand the actual process.

Any time you have questions, or you want to talk about if the homes are not meeting your criteria, have that conversation with your real estate agent.

9. Choose an Agent You Like

There is a lot of trust involved when you are purchasing a home.

You should choose an agent that you enjoy working with but at the end of the day where an agent REALLY earns their weight in salt is... are they a FIERCE NEGOTIATOR!?

You want to pick somebody that you feel is going to look out for your best interest. Find someone you really feel is going to represent you well.

Don't always use the first agent you come across unless you feel this connection with them.

Take some time and ask for referrals. If you need a referral for an agent, call Chris at the number in the footer of this page.

Mortgage Loan Originators can know the best agents because they work with so many in any given year.

Find a real estate agent you really connect with and you feel like you want to work with in this home buying process.

10. It's Important To Understand The Point Of A Home Inspection

Your home inspector is going to be an independent person who probably has never been in the house before.

They are going to have a checklist and it's going to take them several hours to complete this process.

The home inspector, at the end, will provide a written report. Keep in mind, it is their job to find all the little things wrong with the home. Keep perspective. All home, even brand-new ones, have issues. Because you have found a trusted agent at this stage, get their input as to what is mission-critical or what can/should be over looked based on what is important to you.

Keep in mind they will tell you every tiny issue that exists in that home.

While you're going over that report, it's important to know what's important and what's not.

What is a Deal Breaker and what's not, right?

What can you ask the sellers to repair and what could you repair yourself after you move in?

One suggestion is never to ask the seller to repair every item on the inspection checklist. You want to show that you are reasonable and you're not going to ask them to repair the small things that aren't that important that you could easily do yourself when you move in.

11. Keep Your Money Wherever It's At

If you have money in the mattress, you want to get that money in the bank 90 days ahead of when you want to purchase a home.

There's a thing called seasoning and you're going to have to season that money if you want to use it for a down payment or anything that has to do with purchasing a home. Lenders must be able to source funds and 'my mattress' is not an acceptable source. The short version as to why is that buying real estate has been used to launder money in the past so this is a way that lender protect against that. The few ruin it for the many.

If the money is not seasoned the mortgage company will ask you to prove where it came from.

They do not want to see any large deposits into your account without being easily trackable. This of course doesn't include your normal paychecks or child support or any other money that you receive on a monthly basis.

You should also know that the mortgage company will probably look at your bank accounts in the beginning of the transaction but there's also a chance that they could look again right before closing so don't try to be sneaky and add $10,000 to your checking account right before closing.

You could lose the loan approval if they go back and look at your accounts again and see something like that.

12. Start Online, But in The End, Trust A Person

Everybody starts the home buying process online.

They look for homes online, they research different mortgage programs; it's a normal thing these days.

One thing to know is that online information can be outdated or even incorrect. Ever heard someone say, "well it was on the internet, so it must be true..."? Riiigghttt.

There's no requirement or oversight on websites and the information that exists online.

Whatever you find online, in the end, you want to find a *local* professional to help you understand that information and how it pertains to you.

In terms of finding a home, the same thing is true.

Start online with your home search but in the end, you want to find a real estate agent that you trust and work with them.

A local real estate agent is also going to know about homes not available online.

Sometimes, these are referred to as "Pocket Listings" because only a few people know they exist.

Real estate agents will also have relationships with other agents and this can help you find homes that may not be available online.

It may also help you get the contract if you get into multiple offer situations, so it's important to start your search online but in the end trust local professionals. Other agents trust local agents, shouldn't you?

13. Multiple Neighborhood Visits

You want to go to your house and see how it is normally during the day.

Check things like what cars are around, how busy is the neighborhood and what's occurring during a normal work day.

If it's possible, go back around 7 p.m. to see how it is in the evenings.

What is it like when everybody is home from work and school?

What are the neighborhood demographics?

Who do you see in the neighborhood?

Are there kids playing?

Are there people walking in the neighborhood or out enjoying the neighborhood?

What is it like in the evening?

It's also a great idea to go to the property on the weekend to see what is that neighborhood is like on a normal weekend.

What are people doing in that area?

You will get a real feel for the neighborhood by visiting a property during the daytime on a weekday, during the evening on a weekday and on a weekend.

It can sometimes be deceiving only visiting during a weekday when everyone is gone.

14. Write A Love Letter

Alright, we're not talking about to prisoner or to an old high school sweetheart.

In this case we're talking about writing letter to the seller of the home you want to purchase telling them what you love the most about the house.

This letter should be no more than one piece of paper long telling them how you vision your family living in the house.

You want to share things like what excites you about the neighborhood and why you want this transaction to move forward.

This is a great thing to include with an offer especially when you are getting into multiple offer scenarios.

15. Auctions & Bank Sales Can Be Deceiving

Oftentimes you will see people marketing things like pre-foreclosures or short sales or foreclosures, online.

On the surface they can seem like a great deal.

When you really dig in, one of the main differences is these properties are rarely move-in-ready.

Most first-time buyers, especially who have never gone through this process, forget to calculate the cost to rehab the property to make it livable.

So when you're looking for a home and you see these fixer upper specials, keep in mind what else would be required in order to make the foreclosure your family home.

16. When Should I Talk with A Mortgage Loan Originator?

Well, you should talk to a mortgage loan originator is as soon as possible. Seriously. It is never the wrong time to get the right advice, don't you agree?

The thing I have found when I'm talking with any potential home buyer is the first question they ask is, "Who should I talk to and how hard is it to get qualified?"

You want to know if there's going to be any hiccups along the way.

Anything you can do to start that process and talk with your mortgage loan originator as quickly as possible will be helpful so you're not going out there wasting your time.

You don't want to be disappointed to find to find a home you love but can't qualify for and getting pre-approved will prevent that.

Pre-approval – www.FreeScenarioReview.com

17. What Credit Score Do I Need to Get A Mortgage?

It is all about perceived RISK to the lender. The more risk, the less desirable the terms. Period.

Thinks as if you were lending your own money. The less risk you feel the better terms you are likely to provide. More risk... one is likely to make sure they are additionally compensated for that additional risk. Banks do not make decisions personal. Those decisions are all based on statistics and the Law of Large Numbers.

The average credit score one needs to get approved right now is about a 620. Every now and again someone can get a loan in the high 500s. Somewhere between 620-640 is preferable.

Our credit repair partner that you can TRUST has really made some amazing things happen. Ask me for more details about that.

Obviously the higher the score the better, but as we have seen in the past – life happens. Many have credit dings from the past.

There are some benefits to having a higher credit score such as having to bring a lower down payment, lower mortgage insurance [if applicable], lower interest rates, etc. The higher the credit score, obviously, the better.

18. What Will I Look at When You Apply For A Mortgage?

First thing we look at when you're applying for a mortgage is credit. We want to see exactly where you stand credit wise.

Then we want to look at your debt-to-income ratio. We'll see how much debt you're paying compared to your income.

We also look to see if you have any collections.

Sometimes there are some unpaid collections or something on a credit report that people don't realize that they've had. It has been reported that over 1/3 of credit reports have ERRORS! There's a lot of stuff that's on there that people don't realize.

So, it's always good for us to look when you're applying to make sure there's no judgments against you. These things must be paid off before you go and close the loan.

Many times, you have the option to pay them off or at least you can have a payment plan.

We want to make sure that you're back on track to get those things taken care of.

We also look to see if you've had a bankruptcy in the last 7-10 years. That's going to have a determining factor on what's going on when you're applying for the mortgage.

So, all those factors are what we really look at when you apply for a mortgage.

There are many things that show up on credit that you need to be aware of as you look to buy a home. There are other things, like bankruptcies mentioned above, that can thwart your interests regardless of credit score. To see what the things are that have the ability to impact your ability to buy REGARDLESS of your credit score, get the mobile app [www.PocketMortgageAdvice.com].

19. What Does It Mean to Get Pre-Approved For A Home Loan?

It means you have a Mortgage Loan Originator that reviewed your credit, looked at your financial documents, looked everything over and they have determined you meet the guidelines.

So, getting pre-approved is the first step for you to feel comfortable buying a home.

We just talked about what we look at when applying for the mortgage, and once you have given us that information, we can start doing our due diligence.

We take your 'buttoned-up' application and provided back up documentation and compare it to different lender's underwriting guidelines. If there is a match, then a pre-approval is extended and you are out hunting for that perfect home.

20. What Is the Minimum Down Payment to Get A Mortgage?

Well, there are quite a few programs out there.

It's pretty cut and dry with the minimum down payments to get mortgages these days.

There are zero down options with the VA loan and USDA program.

You've also got 3.5% down options with the FHA program.

Conventional loans have options with as low as 3% down.

Those are the three most common down payment options for home loans. The idea of needing 20% down to buy a home is a thing of the past. What a country where you can leverage an appreciating asset to such a high degree and build wealth SLOWLY over time.

If you would like to get an introduction to a financial planner that can help make real estate become incorporated into your overall 'win with money' strategy, just let me know at the email in the footer.

21. How Much Cash Do I Need to Buy A Home?

Well, that depends on exactly what program you're applying and approved for.

Some of the fees most buyers pay at closing include:

- Lender Fees [beware of scams that say there are none.]
- Home appraisal
- Home inspections
- Title closing fees
- Pre-paid taxes and/or insurance
- Third party fees

You will receive a Loan Estimate when you apply for a home loan showing you all the costs with the mortgage company.

22. Should I Pay Discount Points?

Points in of themselves are neither good nor bad. The real question is what benefit they provide and the answer is not always clear.

Many people think that if you want to buy discount or pay discount points to buy down the rate that's going to make a big difference.

You have got to look at the long term, just because you're paying discount points doesn't necessarily mean you're saving money.

You have to figure out how long you will be living in the home. Longevity is the main factor in figuring out if points make sense or not.

This is where you want to get custom advice – not something that can speak to the masses in a book. Call me at the number in the footer if you wish to unpack this topic more.

23. At What Point Is It Worth Paying Discount Points?

Everybody's got a different circumstance so that's why it's important to run a cost savings analysis to see if it makes sense to pay discount points.

It's important to understand what you're trying to accomplish, then we can look at deciding if it makes sense to pay those discount points to get that lower interest rate.

There are a lot of factors involved that should impact your decision on whether to pay discount points.

If it's costing you $5,000 per point on a $400,000 loan; that's a lot of money.

It is smart to do the math and determine if the offset interest you will save by paying the points up front will be worth it in the long term based on your total out of pocket expenses at closing and the length of time you plan to own the home. Again, call me at the number in the footer if you wish to unpack this topic more.

24. What Is the Difference Between A Fixed-Rate Mortgage And ARM Loan?

A fixed rate mortgage stays the same for the entire length of the loan. Nothing changes. So, if you have it for the full term of 10, 15, 20, or 30 years... it stay fixed. [The only thing that might change is your estimates for your tax of insurance.]

Now, for an ARM or Adjustable Rate Mortgage, adjustments can take place after the initial fixed period.

Depending on what ARM program, it might go up or down depending on what the market is doing.

Each type of mortgage has its own benefits, but it is very important that you speak with us and look at each type of loan to see what best fits for your unique situation.

25. What Will My Mortgage Payment Include?

Principal, interest, tax and insurance.

We often abbreviate this as PITI.

Principal - The amount of the loan that you borrowed.

Interest- The charge that the bank or institution charges for lending you the principle.

Tax- The taxes charged by the local and state governments may be included here.

Insurance- The homeowner's insurance (some people call it hazard insurance) this is to cover the home and insure that any problems or damages are able to be covered.

[If applicable] There may be Mortgage Insurance as a part of your payment. That is the 'freight' you pay for the luxury of not putting down 20%. There are ways to avoid this, however. Call me at the number in the footer if you wish to unpack this topic more.

26. Can Someone Give Me Money For My Down Payment?

Yes, they absolutely can.

Often what we see is people's parents that are giving down payment to their kids. You just must make sure you're documenting it. This is commonly done through a 'Gift Letter' from the source of the gift.

Paper trailing this is going to be key to ensure that we understand exactly what those funds are for and that they are to be assigned to the down payment of the home.

27. Why Should I Buy A Home Instead of Rent?

Buying a home is an asset that is likely to appreciate.

You buy a home at $200,000 and hopefully the value goes up as you see the market change and the growth in the area.

Having a home of your own is a financial investment. It's something you're investing in as you pay down the principle.

It's a home AND an investment that can increase in value as you own it. How cool is that?

There are also tax breaks involved so you're able to write certain things off when you are purchasing a home.

Think about it, somebody has even purchased the home or apartment *you* live in. You are paying down the balance on *their* investments and giving them a residual income.

So, there's a big difference compared to renting.

You can't really write anything off when you rent. If there's stuff that you've bought to fix up the house you're renting, you can't write that kind of stuff off on taxes, and that is REAL money!

There are a lot of benefits to owning instead of renting. If you look at anyone that has become 'rich' – chances are there was real estate involved in one form or fashion.

28. How Do I Know How Much House I Can Afford?

That's why we need to talk [phone number in footer] as soon as possible when you are considering becoming a homeowner.

You must have a solid idea of your *usable* income and debts to understand how much you may qualify for on a mortgage.

Speaking with a loan officer sooner rather than later will help you understand where you are currently, and what will be possible in your local housing market.

Generally, you want to have a good understanding of your financial situation *before* you start looking for a home.

We'll calculate everything and figure out exactly what you qualify for, get your proof and then get you out there looking for the house that's perfect for you.

With all those steps in place we can be confident that you will be able to purchase it.

29. How Long Does It Take to Buy A House?

Usually it takes 30 to 45 days from the time you go under contract until you close.

There could be some circumstances that come up that might delay that process but that is a general timeline that most loans are closing in at the moment.

For example, if you purchase a short sale home it might take 3 months to get bank approval and go to closing.

Keep in mind the 30-45 days is from time of agreement with a seller. How long it takes to find the home will depend on inventory and how particular you are. Pre-approval could, depending on how quickly you provide all the needed paperwork, could also take a week or so.

All in, you want to start the process a good 75 - 90 days before you want to move in.

30. What Can I Do If My Credit Is Messed Up?

That's a great question I get all the time about credit. I wouldn't say everybody, but at least 45% of the people that I have financed or helped buy a home over the last 15+ years [a third of my life and growing] have had credit hiccups along the way.

We have a team of real people that have been doing this for folks JUST LIKE YOU for quite some time to help you look at your credit score and get it where it needs to be.

It's important to look at an overall picture of your credit. There may be things on your report that you don't realize are there...happens all the time. There could also be items you had PAID OFF and they were never removed from the report.

There are also situations, like when children are named after their parents, end up getting their credit reports mixed. The names are exact or ALMOST exact and it is easy for the reports to have cross over. This is something to know sooner rather than later, don't you agree?

We have a team of experts who can look that over and be able to get you to where you need to be to get qualified into that 620 - 640 or better range that we talked about earlier.

31. What Is Earnest Money?

Earnest money is the money you put in an escrow account in the beginning to show the seller you are serious about the offer you are making. The more you put into this, the more serious the seller will think you are.

Often a seller just doesn't want to accept anybody's offer that's out there so it's a good faith to prove you are serious about purchasing that person's home.

So, they see you're able to put money down, they know that you're serious and they're willing to possibly accept your offer and get you the closing as quick as possible.

32. Is There A Loan Program Available to Fix Up A House If The House Needs Repairs?

Absolutely. This is a big one throughout the country.

There's a lot of folks looking to find homes and the ones they find need repairs. The houses might have storm damage, be outdated or simply been neglected.

This is what a '203K' type loan is for.

These type loans are one of the ways you can buy a home and borrow money to fix it up the way you want without coming out of pocket.

Ask your Mortgage Loan Originator if the home you want to purchase can qualify for the 203K program.

WARNING: If this is a path you desire to brave... buckle up. It WILL be bumpy, and I will likely have you sign a piece of paper saying you promise we will be friends when it is all said and done.

33. What Is A Home Appraisal?

A home appraisal is a value given to your home by a certified appraiser.

An appraiser is a 3rd party that goes out and appraises the house to give an actual true assessment of what the house is worth based on factors from the objective market. That is not to say that an appraisal is completely objective because part of the appraisal process is as much 'art' as it is 'science'.

Around 2008 there was a big issue that a lot of people were inflating value, so nowadays we take those home appraisals pretty serious.

The appraiser goes out to see what's selling or sold in the area and compare the house you are buying to the other houses within the market to be able to give you a true value of what your home is worth either for a purchase or refinance.

34. Is There A Difference Between Buying A Home to Live In And Buying An Investment Property?

Absolutely. There's a big difference especially in the qualifying process. You can get up to 100% financing when you are looking for a primary residence.

It's more secure that you are purchasing a home and living in it than getting a investment property. You will get better interest rates and higher loan-to-value, so you don't have to bring so much the closing table.

Ultimately this all comes down to risk. There is less risk to a lender on a home you intend to live in than one that is just an investment. Now when you're buying an investment property obviously it's in the name itself, it's an investment, and those require a little bit more money down.

Generally, investment homes require about 20-25% down so be prepared for that.

Occupancy type is one of the biggest variables when it comes to the terms available for a home buyer. Again, it comes down to risk – remember? Is someone more likely to default on a home the live I or one that they rent out? That is what we mean by risk and it is why a primary residence gets better terms than an investment property.

The biggest differences are interest rates and down payment needed at closing.

35. Four Questions to Ask When Buying a Flip

You've seen the pretty pictures online. The beautiful furniture, the open floor plan, stainless steel appliances, it's all new!

A home is considered 'flipped' when an investor buys a home in need of repairs, strips it down and installs a brand-new interior. Sometimes they even install new landscaping and other outdoor features.

First time buyers especially love these 'flipped' homes. Sure, it looks fantastic and you are falling in love, but what's underneath the new facade?

Here's four questions you should ask before closing on this beauty.

What is the home's history?

Everything is public record now, so ask your real estate agent for the transaction history. Why? This will show when the investor bought the home and how much they paid for it.

It will also show the square footage, bedroom and bath count.

An investor might take a patio and create a bedroom or add a shower or even a full bathroom.

As the buyer, you want to know if there's been any plumbing or electrical moved around or added.

Generally, investors are good for housing, yet there are always those that are finks.

Are there any improvements?

Ask the seller for a list of improvements and request them to document it. You want to know where those appliances came from.

This will help you during the inspection period. Especially pay attention to any electrical and plumbing that's been moved, altered or added.

Can you use your inspector?

A licensed property inspector is always a good idea. Make sure you walk around the property with him/her, so they can point out anything that may need further inspection.

I would always get a lateral sewer inspection and have a licensed electrician check the panels. Lots of flippers add more electrical outlets, microwaves and other appliances without upgrading the panel. This is a possible fire hazard and will be expensive to upgrade later.

If you need an inspector referral, pleaseeee let me know. I have folks you can trust.

Where are the permits?

Lots of remodeled homes may have additions without permits. It is not 100% necessary for permits, but any additions should be done in a manner that matches the local code required.

If not, the lender may have issues when the appraisal is done. Ask the seller for the name and license number of the contractor that did the work.

If you have issues later, you have recourse against the contractor. It's a red flag if the work is not done by a contractor.

Not to be a naysayer - a remodeled home CAN be a great purchase!

Everything is done, you move right in and enjoy your new home! Just make sure you know everything about your new home before you close!

36. Condos Are An Affordable Path To Homeownership

Condominiums and townhomes are a great way to enter the homeownership market, but there are some hidden 'gotchas'.

They are typically more affordable in sales price yet the monthly costs on the mortgage can be decentive.

The reason: Association Fees

The monthly association fee for a condo can easily be *several* hundred dollars a month, so compared to a home of the same value your cost of living there will be quite a bit higher. As a general rule, every $1000 you borrow will cost you about $5 a month in a principle and interest payment. That being said, $10,000 would cost about $50 a month, $100,000 would be $500 and so on.

Because of that, you can see that a $250 association fee is like borrowing another $50,000 on a mortgage! In an over simplified example, that would mean a $200,000 condo with a $250 fee, would have the same montly obligation on a $250,000 house with no association fee. You can probably see, even if this is your first time buying a home, those are two *very* different lifestyles.

All that to say, let's jump into some of the other thoughts around a condo or townhome.

The right complex will appreciate as much as a single family neighborhood because once one out paces the other, there is a laso effect that pulls the other along with it. With recent finance changes, condominiums are easier to finance too.

Condominiums and townhomes are an excellent way to start investing in real estate and get out of paying *someone else's* mortgage.

Owning a condo compared to renting? There is no comparison!

With ownership you gain appreciation, equity, tax advantages and the peace of mind you can live there as long as you want. It's truly the only way to control your long term housing expense.

37. What Are Contingencies?

The current purchase contract in Florida is 12-14 pages, there is a lot of information in there!

There are basically 3 contingencies you need to really pay attention to.

If you miss one, you are out of contract, and technically, the seller can cancel your contract and sell your home to someone else... and possibly even *keep* your earnest monies. No bueno.

An experienced agent and lender will make sure you stay on schedule.

The first contingency is the **property inspection**.

The seller usually gives you between 5-15 days to order inspections and satisfy yourself as to the condition of the property.

This is the time you verify the roof doesn't leak, the sewers drain, the electrical systems are adequate and further research any red flags that these inspections discover.

Your agent will go back to the seller accepting the property, ask for repairs, or request things be done poening up further negotiations.

The second contingency is the **appraisal**.

Your lender will order the appraisal as soon as given a green light from you regarding the inspection. One does not want the appraisal ordered if you are still negotiating with the seller for some repairs as it could 'show your hand' and adversely impact your negotiation position. Once all is good, the lender will order the appraisal and it can take about 17 days or so to get the appraisal in and a copy to you. The lender will review the appraisal on your behalf, verify it came in at the sales price and requires no repairs that could impact the financability of the home.

The third and biggest contingency is the **loan contingency**.

When you release this contingency, this means your loan is approved and there is no reason why you cannot buy your new home.

This is where your lender needs to be positive your loan is approved and there is nothing that will cause the loan to be denied. This is typically referred to as a Clear To Close by the lender meaning that though the property has not yet closed, the loan is fully completed and the borrower (you) is fully approved.

In a seller's market, contingencies are a great way to make your offer better than others, without paying a higher price.

Is it very easy to shorten timelines?

Shorter timelines are valuable to a seller at times and may increase the odds of your offer being accepted.

Is it risky? Not, if done right.

An experienced agent and lender *team* will ensure you will not risk losing your deposit if timelines aren't met. This is one of many reasons you benfit from working with and agent and a lender that have a track record of working together and not a la carting these things together on your own.

In this case, the appraisal gets ordered right away, sometimes on a rush (which can cost extra).

The inspections need to be done within a few days.

We sometimes don't even write in a loan contingency, making the buyer equal to a cash buyer.

How do we do that? We fully underwrite and pre-approve the buyer BEFORE the offer is accepted. Not all lenders can or will do this so if it is important to you, be sure you are working with someone like us that can.

38. Explore Your Down Payment Options

When buying a home, you basically need two piles of money.

One is for the down payment and the other is for the associated costs for closing.

Generally, closing costs are 3% of the sales price yet your down payment will vary, depending on the loan type. You can get a great mortgage calculator APP for your smart phone by visiting www.PocketMortgageAdvice.com

If you're using VA home loan benefits, you will not need a down payment, otherwise, consider these options.

401K Loan –

If you have a 401K, TSP or other retirement account, you should ask the plan administrator if you can take out a loan specifically for the purposes of buying a home. Most plans allow you to borrower 50% of the balance and can usually set the interest rate and payment.

It is not a taxable event because it's not a withdrawal, you *borrow* the money from yourself.

How cool is that? The lender will not count the payment against you and lower your approval amount.

IRA's do not usually allow for a loan and can only be a withdrawal.

Down Payment Assistance (DPA) –

Grants are available through cities, counties and states. A grant does not show up on your property and in some cases, does not have to be repaid. Be careful, however, because you are surely 'getting in bed with the government'. It can be harder to get your offers accepted and there can be tremendous amounts of red-tape to navigate around.

The costs of borrowing the money with DPA can also be quite a bit more with much higher rates of interest.

Most grants can cover the down payment and closing costs. This should be a last resort. If you absolutely *need* it to buy a home – by all means explore this option. If it just sounds great because it sounds like 'free money' dig deeper and uncover all the other things that really show that it can be more hassle than it is ultimately worth.

Lender Credits –

Technically, you cannot use lender credits for a down payment. You can, however, use the credits for closing costs, saving your cash *for* the down payment.

If you leverage a credit from your lender, understand, there is no magic there. TO 'create' the extra monies to offset your costs, the lender needs to charge you a higher interest rate. You will need to look at all interest rate options to see if the higher rate is worth the extra cash at closing. This *can* be a serious win when looking at it as a 'bang for your buck' standpoint. Have your lender explain the trade-off and give you your breakeven point. The BE point will let you know whether it is an advantageous exchange or not.

Gift Funds –

You can buy a home with zero money out of pocket if you find a supportive relative to give you the cash. It's OK if you intend to *occupy* your new home.

The best way to utilize gift funds is allowing your donor to leave their money in their own bank account and them wire it to the title company a day or so before the closing.

The lender will simply ask for a copy of the donor's bank statement and a letter stating this money does not have to be repaid.

Borrow From an Asset –

You can borrow money on an asset if you can afford another payment in your debt ratio.

Many buyers can refinance their car if it's owned free and clear. This is an excellent way to get cash for your home purchase.

There have been recent changes in lending allowing for lower down payments, so make sure you speak with an experienced loan origination team who can create a financing package that helps you meet your real estate objectives and make sure it fits in your overall financial goals. The time has passed where a mortgage can be seen as a stand alone transaction – it truly needs to be viewed from a higher level and contribute to your overall 'Win With Money' strategy.

39. Let's Talk About Sewers & Septics

It's a fact, every home must have a sewer drain if it is not on a septic system.

There's basically two types. A public sewer takes all the waste water from your home into the main sewer pipes under the street.

If you live in a rural area where no public sewer is available, you will have a septic tank. This is a giant tank buried in your yard where the wastewater goes and must be pumped out occasionally.

Nationally, public sewers are most common so we will speak mostly to these.

When purchasing a home, a lateral sewer inspection is highly recommended. During the inspection phase of your purchase, you can contract a licensed plumber to send a camera down through the main drain. The camera will show, through a video, exactly what is clear or blocked all the way to the main sewer line in the street.

This can be a particularly big problem when buying an investor remodeled home, or a flip.

Generally, flippers are known for cutting corners though there are some really good and integrous ones. For example, when a flipper demolishes a home, if they do not cover the hole where the toilet goes, all the construction debris can clog up the pipes. If they then set a new toilet over it and never verify the drains are clear... boom... you got a problem. A normal property inspection does not discover this.

Once the unsuspecting buyer moves in and starts using all the plumbing, the construction debris can catch somewhere in the plumbing and cause sewage back ups anywhere there is a drain. Eww.

This is not pleasant!

Another main reason for back ups is tree roots.

When the inspection camera goes through the line, you will be able to see all the dirt, cracks and roots that can block the main line. Since it's lateral, it does not really drain downhill and can easily clog with debris. This is the time you would show the video to the seller and request repairs or renegotiate a change satisfactory to both parties.

Don't find yourself on the wrong end of a clogged drain, get an inspection.

40. Attention Military - Top 5 Reasons You Want To Use Your VA Loan Benefit

If you've served our country by being in the military, you deserve this awesome benefit!

In most cases, it is the best loan out there.

VA loans offer no down payment, low rates, no mortgage insurance and generous underwriting guidelines.

Let's look at the top 5 reasons you should use your VA home loan benefit.

No Down Payment –

The national loan amount is close to a half million dollars.

This means anywhere in the country, you can buy a home using VA financing with zero money down.

In high cost counties, mostly metropolitan areas, the max loan amount can be higher.

No PMI –

With other loan types, unless you bring in 20% cash down payment, your lender will require you to buy Private Mortgage Insurance. There is no *direct* benefit to the home buyer for this so if it can be avoided (there are a few ways to do this, actually, so ping us with your questions) you may want to do so.

The VA loan program is paid for with a funding fee, a one time cost added to the loan. AND, if you have at least a 10% service related disability, even *this* fee will be waived.

This saves the average home buyer several hundred dollars a month on the payment.

Generous Credit Guidelines –

VA loans are the only home loans that allow you to buy a home 2 years after a major derogatory event like bankruptcy, foreclosure and short sale.

You are also not penalized as heavily for having low credit scores. A 620 FICO score can still get you a good rate. Other loan programs require a minimum 680 to be competitive.

Qualify For a Higher Loan Amount –

Most lenders use a debt ratio to determine your ability to repay a mortgage. Not the VA! VA loans use a residual income model. This benefits most military buyers and helps them qualify for substantially more than with other programs.

Better Interest Rates –

VA loans usually carry a lower interest rate than other programs.

Conventional loans want you to have a 720 minimum score or you will pay a substantially higher rate.

Some lender claim they can use a 580 score, but it can be really expensive!

You're better off to take a few months and improve your score before buying. Most VA lenders use a 620 score to get a good rate and 680+ to do a little better.

VA loans can be used more than once. Sometimes even before the original loan is paid off.

Your best bet is to talk to an experienced VA lender, like us, who can share their knowledge and direct you to an experienced agent.

The teamwork of a good agent/lender will ensure your offer gets accepted, your timelines met, and have you moving into your home on time.

41. 15 Year Mortgage vs 30 Year Mortgage

Many times throughout the week I get asked, "What is the difference between a 15-year mortgage and a 30-year mortgage"?

I usually try and lighten up the mood a little and respond with a quick, "About 15 years or 180 monthly payments!"

Really what my borrower is trying to determine is, does it make more financial sense to sign closing papers on a 15-year mortgage or a 30-year mortgage?

So, the question I ask is, "What are you trying to accomplish by getting a 15-year loan verses a 30-year loan"?

Most of the time the answer to this question is that they just want to pay the loan off quicker than 30 years.

I am 100% fine with either loan, the borrower needs to evaluate a few key pieces to buying this home to make sure they make the right choice.

Using a robust mortgage calculator (www.PocketMortgageAdvice.com) can easily answer if this makes financial sense for you.

For a simple illustration, we will use a loan amount of $250,000 with a 4% interest rate for a 30-year note and a 3.75% interest rate for a 15-year note.

This is just an example and not a guarantee that either of these interest rates are attainable at the time of reading this book. For context, the average rate over the last 60 years has been 8.375%.

If we take the $250,000 loan amount with these interest rates we will quickly determine that the principal and interest payment for the 30-year note is $1194, and the payment for the 15-year note is $1818, a monthly difference of $624.

The second piece we need to consider is where might we put that other $624 to *earn* interest? A sound financial advisor is worth their weight in gold and if you do not have someone – not realated by blood – that you look to for financial advice, let me know and I will gladly introduce you to someone that has been vetted already and can surely offer you sound counsel.

I am not guaranteeing any rate on return from an investment.

When using an investment calculator and entering in our $624 monthly difference for 15 years, the time difference between the 30-year note and the 15-year note.

If you use an average rate of return of 6%. **Again, I am not guaranteeing any rate on return from an investment.** After 15 years of making this investment at this rate of return you would find you would have $175,785.91 in your investment account.

Going back to the mortgage, after 15 years of paying my minimum monthly payment on a 30 year mortgage, the balance is $161,357. One could write a check, from that investment account, for the entire amount and still have over $14,000 left. The point is there are *two* sides to interest – interest you pay and interest you earn. Don't forget about the other side of earning interest even though it is easy to do so.

The financially disciplined borrower can take the difference and invest it into a non-qualified, diversified, mutual fund account with a good financial coach and have access to the money if and when you need it. That is an additional benefit... YOU stay in control of your own money and can access it if something in life goes sideways on you. This is infinitely more conservative and safer for a homeowner than committing to a high monthly payment.

Signing the 30-year note will allow you to build up some additional wealth and should something happen, you now have access to the funds needed to do unforeseen repairs.

In the event you already have a sizeable non-qualified account to pull from maybe the 15-year mortgage is the best way to go, yet be sure to get good, sound counsel.

42. More Money Down?

A couple times a month I will get asked questions about putting more money down on a home instead of the minimum requirement.

Usually this is a situation where a borrower has either saved up money specifically because someone told them they must put 20% down.

Sometimes this question comes up because someone wants to close out an old retirement account and utilize that money for a down payment.

I like to utilize math and financial wisdom to see how best to advise a borrower.

Let's pretend that you have saved up $50,000 for your down payment, because you thought you needed that much.

That would provide for you a $250,000 sales price on your home ($50,000 = 20% of $250,000).

Using the mobile mortgage APP calculator at www.PocketMortgageAdvice.com, one can start with that previously referenced $250,000 purchase with 20% down creating a $200,000 loan amount at 4% on a 30-year mortgage.

That quickly shows us that a monthly payment for principal and interest would be $955.

To compare, use the calculation on an FHA loan with the minimum down payment of 3.5% creating a $241,250 loan amount.

Our payment is now $197 *more* per month.

The answer to whether the borrower should invest the extra money depends on their *whole* financial picture. Remember there are TWO kinds of interest, right? The kind you pay and the kind you earn.

If you took that same $41,250 that you have now *not* used as down payment and put it in a shoebox under your bed, each month you could go grab the extra $197 to pay your mortgage payment and you would have money in that shoe box for over 209 months, that's over 17 years, to use for other things in the case of an emergency or change in priority!

If you placed it in a conservative investment rather than a shoe box and it was earning a 3% rate of return on that $41,250, that would give us $68,179.96 after those same 17 years. (If we left it alone for the full 30 years that we pay on our mortgage we would have over $100,000!) Wow.

So, a good rule of thumb is to realize that on average you will only save about $5 per month for every $1000 that you put down on the mortgage.

Is it worth saving $5 per month?

The answer is completely up to you yet I encourage you to think about your whole money picture not the mortgage as a stand alone transaction. Do you need that financial advisor introduction that can unpack this a bit further? Just let me know.

I have had many people put the extra money down because they had saved the money for this specific purpose and they know their monthly budget will allow the payment at the lower amount.

They usually fear that if they choose to keep the money they will spend it on something else and their monthly budget will be out of tune. That is a legit reason to distance the money from yourself. The strategy previously spelled out doesn't work if you infuse those other dollars into your lifestyle.

I have also had many families decide to use that money to start an investment account with a local financial advisor and treat the purchase of their home like an investment tool. Smart.

43. Do You Like To Gamble?

Throughout each month I am probably asked a million times, "Well, what is the interest rate?"

Here is the amusing piece to that question, if I were to ask someone what the interest rate on their home is currently, 80% have no idea!

This is only a question that matters when financing the home.

So naturally a follow up question usually is, "What would you like it to be?"

Our local market is pretty competitive and most mortgage bankers in this area have virtually the same rates, so shopping for an interest rate usually doesn't make up for the time spent shopping.

After all, isn't the purpose of a lower rate to be a lower monthly payment?

Here is where I let, you, the borrower make a choice.

Do you like to gamble?

We can look at rates all the way down at the bottom of the spectrum, it only means if you want that rate, you better be willing to pay for it! Imagine closing costs and interest rate are on the opposite side of the same see-saw. As one goes down, what happens to the other?

So what does gambling have to do with anything?

Well if you 'pay' for a lower interest rate we need to determine when you will make up that investment.

Let's define a term really quick.

A "discount point" is 1% of the loan amount. On a $200,000 loan, that would equate to $2,000.

So, 2 points would be 2%. When buying down a interest rate you *use* discount points. For example, back when you could easily get rates in the 4s, you could secure a 3.75% rate yet it could cost you 1.35 discount points, or 1.35% of the loan amount or $2,700 in additional closing costs.

For the next few minutes let's create a fresh scenario.

We found a perfect home for $235,000. We will utilize a 3.5% down payment program to give us a loan amount of $226,775 ($235,000 – 3.5% ($8,225) = $226,775)

A quick jump to the calculator you now have on your phone, will show you that the difference between a 4.25% and 4.125% is between $16 and $17 per month.

Let's make an assumption that for every .125% of an interest rate the associated fee is half of a point or .5% in discount points.

So for our scenario a 4.25% interest rate would cost you $0 in discount points, but for a 4.125% (an .125 difference) it would cost you half a point, or $1133.87.

Are you with me so far?

Now we need to determine how many months of saving our $16-$17 per month it will take to recover the initial cost. THIS is called the Break Even Point and is what I eluded to earlier in the book.

So for our mathematicians out there, we take the difference in payment from the original payment to the new payment ($1116-$1099 = $17).

The we divide that into the cost of the buy down to determine months to make up payment ($1133.88 / $17 = 66.70).

So, for us to invest $1133.88 up front it would take us 66.70 months or just over 5.5 years to recover the $1133.88 at a rate of $16-17 a month.

So, do you like to gamble? Will you be in this same loan for more than 5.5 years?

Here is a quick table of what the fee would be to "buy down" the interest rate and the number of months it would take to recover that fee based on our example:

This is not a guarantee of what the discount fees cost, this is just an example.

Loan Amount	$226,775			
Rate	price	cost	payment	month to make up payment
4.250%	0	$ -	$1,116	0.00

4.125%	0.5%	$1,133.88	$1,099	66.70
4.000%	1%	$2,267.75	$1,083	68.72
3.875%	1.5%	$3,401.63	$1,066	68.03
3.750%	2%	$4,535.50	$1,050	68.72
3.625%	2.5%	$5,669.38	$1,034	69.14
3.500%	3%	$6,803.25	$1,018	69.42

44. How Can I Best Be Prepared To Get A Home Loan

I saw, one time, a friend in the mortgage business that had on the back of his business card, the 10 Commandments of Home Buying. What a great idea, as it could be a very resourceful tool to anyone looking to get ready to buy a home.

Here they are:

1. Thou shalt not change jobs, become self-employed or quit your current job.

2. Thou shalt not buy a car, truck or van, or other large 'machine / toy' (or you may be living in it!)

3. Thou shalt not use credit cards excessively or let current accounts fall behind.

4. Thou shalt not spend money you have set aside for closing costs or down payment.

5. Thou shalt not omit debts or liabilities from your loan application.

6. Thou shalt not buy furniture on credit.

7. Thou shalt not originate any additional inquiries on your credit.

8. Thou shalt not make large deposits without checking with me first.

9. Thou shalt not change bank accounts.

10. Thou shalt not co-sign for a loan with anyone.

I think some of these are fairly obvious why you shouldn't do them, but let's break them down just to make sure.

1. Thou shalt not change jobs, become self-employed or quit your job.

Most loan programs require a minimum of 30 days on a job, as long as you have been in that same line of employment, or education for that position before you can get a loan. The longer you have been employed in the same line of work the stronger the file. If you jump to self-employment, you need 2 years' worth of tax returns to verify income, so you may have just thwarted your own interests if you do that *while* buying a home or as you are getting ready to.

2. Thou shalt not buy a car, truck or van (or you may be living in it!).

Not only will this drop your credit score due to the number of auto loan inquiries, but it could also increase your payment on this liability and knock you out of being able to purchase.

3. Thou shalt no use credit cards excessively or let current accounts fall behind.

The underwriting team will always pull credit as your approach closing to insure debts, and monthly obligations have not increased.

4. Thou shalt not spend money you have set aside for closing costs or down payment.

The loan officer will turn in bank statements to show stability of savings account and proof of funds to close, if you spend that money you can rest assured that your loan will not close on time.

5. Thou shalt not omit debts or liabilities from your loan application.

This is basically lying about debts. If you omit them, when the debt is discovered the underwriting team will question why it was omitted and the loan process will start over. It will also taint other information provided and the whole file will be reviewed with more scrutiny.

6. Thou shalt not buy furniture on credit.

Just wait until you close on the house. Most of the time this is done because you get such a great deal and save 10% by 'purchasing today'. When shopping for new furniture, just tell the sales person, "I am closing on my house in a few weeks and cannot buy today, I am just looking."

7. Thou shalt not originate any additional inquiries on your credit.

New inquiries on credit makes underwriters think there is new debt or that there may be financial strain.

8. Thou shalt not make large deposits without checking with me first.

Large deposits are always suspicious. Check with us to see what the definition of large deposit is on the loan program you are using for your home purchase.

9. Thou shalt not change bank accounts.

Why would you want to change banks in the middle of the largest financial transaction of your life? If you hate your current bank that much, change after we close on your new home.

10. Thou shalt not co-sign for a loan with anyone.

Co-signing on a loan now makes you liable for that loan as well. IN other words, there is no such thing as co-signing... just signing. You are 100% liable for a loan you co-sign on. No difference. So now we must start over with this new debt on your application.

45. Prepare Early & Seek The Advice Of A Trusted Mortgage Advisor

When buying a home, you want to make sure everything is lined up the best you possibly can.

Do not start shopping, or even, looking at homes until you have a few pieces of information lined up.

First, identify what is your maximum comfortable monthly payment, including taxes and insurance, that your budget will allow.

Knowing this number is more important than knowing how much of a house you can qualify to buy.

If your maximum monthly payment is $2,000 you will not be able to buy a $500,000 home.

Different loan programs have different guidelines on how much you can pay for your mortgage based on the amount of income you earn.

This is called your front debt to income ratio.

The goal here is to establish a price range of homes that you will feel comfortable with paying each month.

After you have determined what your monthly budget will allow in a payment, start gathering a few needed documents.

I recommend starting a file folder on your computer, or paper copy if you prefer.

Start saving items to this file so that you can quickly upload them to the loan file electronically or email them to your loan officer.

Every loan program will need 2 years worth of tax returns with all W2s used to determine the income. Having enlarged color copies of your driver's license and social security cards are much easier to read.

We will need 30 days worth of paycheck stubs from everyone on the loan application. If you get paid every 2 weeks, keep in mind, this will be three pay stubs since 2 will only cover 28 days.

We will need the past 2 months bank statements.

Ideally this is a checking and savings account where the money for closing is kept.

List out the last 2 years of employment with the name of the company, address and who to contact for verification.

Have this for your past 2 years of residence history as well.

If you are applying for a VA loan, there are other documents needed like your DD-214 and Certificate of Eligibility.

If you are paying or receiving child support we will need the documents showing a current status, especially if you are using this as part of your income on the application.

Sometimes people chose to use some of the funds from their 401(k) for down payment and closing coast, if that is you then you'll need to provide those statements as well.

Finally, if you are receiving social security or disability income, we would need the documents showing the monthly amount received.

Being prepared makes your job much simpler, as well as the job for your loan origination team.

Utilize the file folder recommendation mentioned earlier and send only what is needed at the time you sign the home purchase contract. You should also understand that delays in receiving needed documents could delay the loan process.

46. Be Smart Around Home Owner's Insurance

Insurance is the "transfer of risk for a fee". This is most commonly referred to as the premium.

There are many games played in insurance and a common one is presenting that all insurance is equal. All things being equal – cheaper is better, right? The devil is in the details. Decisions are frequently made based on a "Declarations Page" which could be a simple page or two of the coverage high points. Well, when you *get* the actual policy, it is more like 52 pages than just the 2 a decision was based on. That is where they "win the business" by having the cheapest premium, only to have insurance that won't be there when you need it. Be careful!

It is much more important that an insurance company pay your claim if you experience a loss. Things to be sure to consider beyond premium are; coverage, deductibles, service, and exclusions.

These all need to be a part of the decision-making process. As a side note, the exclusions are frequently in the buried language also called 'the fine print'.

It is easy for the agency to artificially reduce or increase the premium based on many factors including *how* the property was quoted. It is critical that the home be quoted honestly and accurately to make certain that if you have a claim, it will not be denied due to a mistake or misrepresentation on the quote. At the end of the day YOU sign the application for insurance so if it is wrong, it is on you for material misrepresentation and likely the reason a claim would be denied.

Remember, insurance companies are for-profit companies and will not pay a claim if they believe that they were deceived or misled. Intentionally or unintentionally.

You worked very hard to purchase your home. It may be your largest asset. Do not let your guard down by simply buying the least expensive policy that you can find without considering the other factors we mentioned.

Bottom line – find an insurance company you can TRUST.

47. Home Security

Having a home Security Systems in the 21st Century is a lot different than it was even just a decade ago. We are living in a world of "SMART technology", and the consumer can manage their busy lives much easier.

Having a Smart Home Security system today gives you the ability to monitor and manage your lives much easier right from the palm of our hand. Instead of paying expensive fees to your cable provider for a phone line that you don't use anymore, you can get an APP on your phone that does it all! These alarm APPs are cheaper than a phone line and they are safer because there no wires to cut.

Having an APP on your phone also gives you the ability to monitor who is coming and going and it sends you open & close reports directly to your smart device. That's not all, Smart Home Security APPs have many bells and whistles. These APPs have ability to control your thermostat, lights, and can set your alarm system right from your phone REGARDLESS of where you are. If you want interior or exterior cameras, you can connect those as well and watch - in real time - what is going on in your home.

There are so many alarm systems today that have the Smart Home Security features and some of them even have ability to have two-way voice systems. If you have your arms full of groceries or your carrying a child and you can't get to the touch screen keypad, a live operator will come on and ask you for your verbal pass code. If they don't get a verified response from you, police are dispatched immediately.

Alarm Systems aren't just about robbers anymore. These alarm systems help in real life emergencies. Whether it be a fire, police or medical emergency, having a Smart Home Security System in your home just makes sense.

Remember Your Local Alarm Dealer is there to help you and your family make decisions about the best systems for you and your family in today's changing world of technology.

"PROTECT WHAT YOU LOVE".

Conclusion

In conclusion, I think the biggest thing when anybody is purchasing a home is to get pre-approved first.

What most people think is that they need to talk to a Realtor first. They want to go ask the Realtor a ton of questions about the home buying process and neighborhoods and payments when they haven't even found if they can qualify for a mortgage.

I tell people, "The best thing to do before you go and get yourself all excited on the internet looking at all these homes you want to purchase, you've got to make sure that you're qualified first. Do that before you get in a Realtor's car and have them showing you homes."

So, that's why you need to go ahead and talk with your Loan Officer as quick as possible.

Find out what you qualify for, get a pre-approval letter and then you're off to the races to purchase your home.

Are You Ready To Get Sound **Security** Advice To Protect Your Home?

Reach out and let's chat...

Shawnie Whitaker

407.543.2060

Shawnie.Whitaker@Home-Security-Ninja.com

www.ingramcontent.com/pod-product-compliance
Lightning Source LLC
Chambersburg PA
CBHW071206220526
45468CB00002B/514